BEDTIME
WORDS

Jenny Tyler
Illustrated by Sue Stitt

With consultant advice from John Newson and Gillian Hartley of the Child Development Research Unit at Nottingham University, and Robyn Gee.

Designed by Kim Blundell and Mary Cartwright

bath

potty

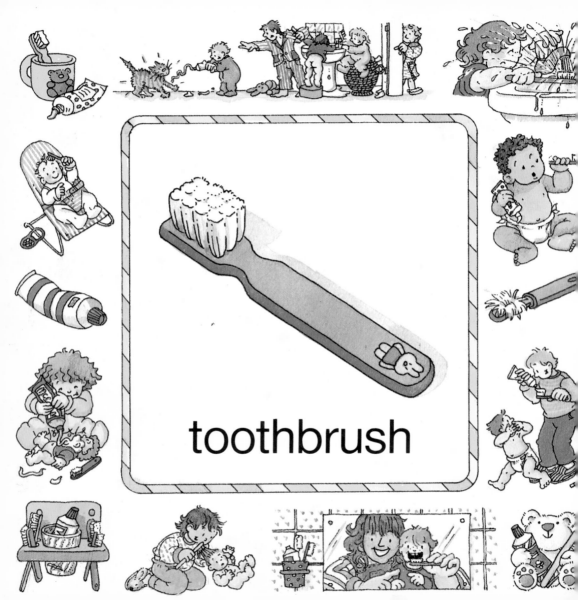

toothbrush

clock

teddy

book

stairs

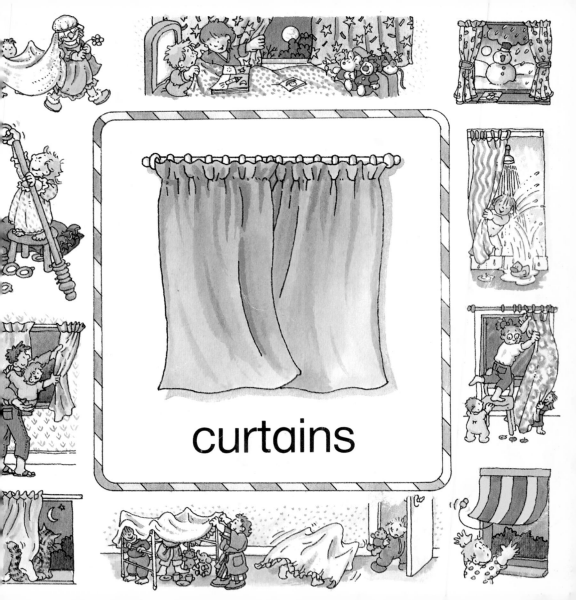

curtains

bed

light

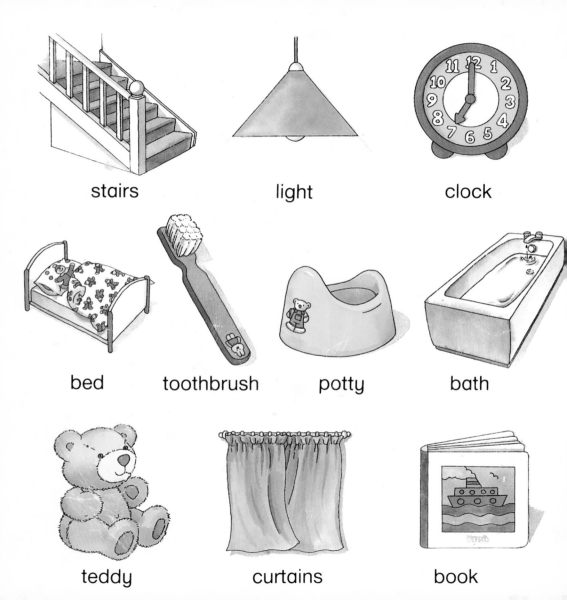

stairs

light

clock

bed

toothbrush

potty

bath

teddy

curtains

book